D0926480

Living a Healthy Lifestyle

Toney Allman

ReferencePoint Press®

San Diego, CA

For more information, contact:
ReferencePoint Press, Inc.
PO Box 27779
San Diego, CA 92198
www.ReferencePointPress.com

LIBRARY OF CONGRESS CATALOGING-IN-PUBLICATION DATA

Name: Allman, Toney, author.
Title: Living a Healthy Lifestyle/by Toney Allman.
Description: San Diego, CA: ReferencePoint Press, Inc., 2020. | Series: Teen Life Skills | Audience:
   Grade 9 to 12. | Includes bibliographical references and index.
Identifiers: LCCN 2019014174 (print) | LCCN 2019015326 (ebook) | ISBN 9781682827468 (eBook)
   | ISBN 9781682827451 (hardback)
Subjects: LCSH: Teenagers—Health and hygiene—Juvenile literature. | Health behavior in
   adolescence—Juvenile literature.
Classification: LCC RA777 (ebook) | LCC RA777 .A46 2020 (print) | DDC 613/.0433—dc23
LC record available at https://lccn.loc.gov/2019014174

CONTENTS

What Is a Healthy Lifestyle?

The constitution of the World Health Organization states, "Health is a state of complete physical, mental and social well-being and not merely the absence of disease or infirmity."[1] Health is a condition of being that keeps you feeling fit and well while giving you the ability to bounce back from illness or injury. A healthy lifestyle is one that improves or maintains health and well-being and lowers the risk of becoming seriously ill or dying early.

Healthy living is as important for teens as it is for any age group. In some ways it is even more important. Excepting the first year of a human's life, no other age group experiences more growth than teens. They are growing rapidly—physically, cognitively, and emotionally. This is why so many teens are hungry all the time. Chris Hudson, an Australian parenting coach, recalls, "I can distinctly remember that time of life when I could come home from school eat nearly a loaf of bread and peanut butter and still be hungry 2 hours later at dinner—all without getting fat."[2] Such appetites are normal because of the growth spurts that teens experience. Growth is also a large part of why teenagers are exhausted much of the time. Many drag themselves up for school each day and then want to sleep the weekends away. They are not being lazy; their growth spurts increase the need for sleep. During this unique period of life, good lifestyle habits can ensure optimal health and growth.

Lifestyle habits developed during youth also have a major lifelong impact. Heart disease in adults, for example, often has its beginnings during the teen years. Many teens who have poor nutritional and sleep habits, use nicotine or marijuana, and make other unhealthy behavioral choices are putting themselves at risk for heart problems later in life. Medical experts do not know for certain who will develop serious heart disease. However, Elizabeth Cespedes Feliciano, a research scientist at health care provider Kaiser Permanente in California, says, "But

> "Health is a state of complete physical, mental and social well-being and not merely the absence of disease or infirmity."[1]
>
> —World Health Organization constitution

These young cyclists are getting the kind of exercise that will help them stay healthy and fit.

we do know from prior studies that habits formed during adolescence and also cardiometabolic risk factors [risk for heart disease and diabetes] established during adolescence can increase the risk of [heart] disease later in life."[3]

Strong bones in old age are dependent on the lifestyle habits of the teen years, too. Bone growth peaks during puberty and the teen years. The healthier bones are during this time, the less likely individuals are to develop osteoporosis in their later years. Osteoporosis is a disease in which bone mass is lost, and bone weakness leads to serious fractures. According to the National Institutes of Health, "The health habits . . . kids are forming now can make, or literally break, their bones as they age."[4]

It can be hard for most teens to think about their future health. Problems like heart disease or osteoporosis seem very far away. Nevertheless, health experts urge young people to care about lifelong health. Psychologist Thomas G. Plante says that young people often believe that they can do what they want now and choose a healthier lifestyle later. He explains, however, that lifestyle habits developed during the teen years are extremely hard to change, warning, "So, take health habits seriously at a young age. It will make a difference in the long term for health, well-being, and longevity."[5]

A healthy lifestyle during the teen years not only protects your future, it also makes for a healthier, happier, more energetic present. Healthy teens improve their learning abilities, enhance self-confidence, are better able to maintain a positive psychological outlook, and just enjoy life more. A healthy lifestyle is really a way to love yourself.

CHAPTER ONE

Nutrition and a Healthy Diet

A healthy lifestyle, almost by definition, requires good nutrition. For teens and young adults, a nutritious diet and eating a healthy balance of appropriate foods are particularly important, both for their bodies and for their brains.

Your Brain on Food

The rapid physical growth of younger teens makes it obvious that they need the nutrients to support that growth, but even older teens, whose growth has slowed, have an increased need for nutritious foods. The brain continues to develop and grow through the teen years, and this development is not complete until about age twenty-five. During this time of brain maturation, the prefrontal cortex—the part of the brain that controls reasoning and judgment—continues to develop. The American Academy of Child & Adolescent Psychiatry adds, "Other changes in the brain during adolescence include a rapid increase in the connections between the brain cells and making the brain pathways more effective. Nerve cells develop myelin, an insulating layer that helps cells communicate."[6] Every cell in the brain (as well as throughout the body) requires nutrients, both to process and transmit information correctly and to grow.

Dr. Neville Golden, a specialist in adolescent medicine at Stanford University School of Medicine, says, "If [teens] don't eat right, they can become irritable, depressed [and] develop problems such as obesity and eating disorders."[7] He explains that good nutrition can help ease or prevent such mental difficulties. The kinds of foods young people eat can directly affect how they feel and function. Good nutrition optimizes a person's ability to focus and pay attention, which is especially important for learning new skills. It increases memory ability, too, so for academic success, a well-fed brain is important. Mood, happiness, interest in fun activities, and energy are all dependent to a large degree on giving the developing brain what it needs.

> "Teens need more nutrients than anyone."[8]
>
> —Heather Mangieri, dietitian

Teens and young adults need to care about eating a balanced diet most of the time, even if they indulge in unhealthy food choices occasionally. Dietitian Heather Mangieri of the Academy of Nutrition and Dietetics explains, "No single food will cause harm to the brain, but there are certainly some foods that are considered beneficial for brain health. The most important consideration for . . . teenagers is that the brain is fed." She adds, "Teens need more nutrients than anyone."[8]

Nutrition Needs

So what is good nutrition for teens? First, they must get enough calories for energy. For teen males, on average, this means about 2,800 calories a day, and 2,200 calories for teen females. Most of these calories should come from healthy foods. Protein—often from meat, dairy products, and fish—is perhaps the most critical nutrient for brain growth and development. Vegetarian teens can satisfy their protein needs through dairy products, soy products, beans, and nuts. Protein is necessary for the growth and development of the body and the brain, as well as the production of hormones. Foods high in proteins help produce the hormones that signal the brain that you are full. This has the advantage of

A healthy diet includes plenty of fruits and vegetables, which supply important nutrients such as vitamins and minerals.

helping people not overeat, so protein foods can help keep people at a healthy weight, too. Teens need from 45 to 60 grams of protein daily, which is equivalent to about 6 ounces of meat for boys and 5 ounces for girls. (Three ounces of meat is roughly the size of a deck of playing cards.)

Animal foods are also a rich source of iron, a mineral for which teens have a dramatically increased need. Iron helps the blood carry oxygen to all parts of the body, including the brain. Mangieri says, "Iron deficiency is one of the most common nutrient deficiencies across the life span. If you're not getting enough, you run the risk of not being able to focus or concentrate."[9]

In addition to protein, teens require daily consumption of healthy fats, complex carbohydrates, and fruits and vegetables for their vitamin and mineral content. Healthy fats are found in foods such as eggs, nuts, olive oil, salmon, and avocados. The fats in avocados, for example, have been shown to increase blood flow to the brain. Complex carbohydrates are a primary source

Don't Fall for That Fad Diet

Fad diets may be the latest thing and very popular, but they are best avoided. Such weight loss diets promise dramatic results in a short amount of time. Examples of fad diets include ketogenic diets, paleo diets, juice cleansing diets, and diets that require fasting. They are often unhealthy, depend on water loss for quick results, achieve only temporary weight loss, and may even be nutritionally dangerous. To spot a fad diet, Boston Children's Hospital suggests asking yourself these questions:

- Does this diet make some foods completely off-limits?
- Does this diet promise that I'll lose an unrealistic amount of weight in a short amount of time? For example: "ten pounds in one week."
- Does the diet refer to food as "good" or "bad"?
- Do I have to buy certain foods for this diet at a special store?
- Does this claim I can lose weight "without exercising"?
- Is this plan temporary?

If the answer to any of these questions is yes, it is probably a fad diet.

Young Men's Health, "Fad Diets vs. Healthy Weight Management," Division of Adolescent and Young Adult Medicine at Boston Children's Hospital, August 17, 2017. https://young menshealthsite.org.

of energy for both the body and the brain. They can be found in whole grains, such as whole wheat bread, oatmeal, popcorn, brown rice, beans, and vegetables. Simple carbs are basically sugars and are not as good for the brain. Simple carbs are found in foods like sugar, candy, white breads and baked goods, corn syrup, fruit juices made from concentrates, and soda. Simple carbs do provide energy, but they do not provide all the nutrients of complex carbs and are not as filling. Eating too many simple carbs can encourage unhealthy weight gain because you get hungry again more quickly. The sugars in sodas and other sweet drinks have also been found to interfere with the way the body absorbs and uses calcium, and teens need as much calcium as they can get for developing healthy bones. Fruits and vegetables, with all the vitamins and minerals they contain, aid brain and body growth, too. Nutritionists recommend that teens eat about two cups of fruits and three cups of vegetables each day. Studies have shown that eating foods such as blueberries, strawberries, and a variety of vegetables improves thinking skills, memory, and decision-making ability.

Achieving a Balanced Diet

Deciding what kinds of foods to eat for a healthy body and brain can seem complex and tedious, but it doesn't have to be. Dietitian and nutrition coach Alissa Rumsey understands that nutrition can seem confusing. She reports that "52% [of] people say figuring out how to eat a healthy diet is more difficult than completing a tax return." Rumsey says that a healthy diet is a balanced diet that does not depend on one food for health or forbid another as bad. She believes getting the right amount of nutrients from foods can be simple. She advises, "Focus on whole foods—i.e. eat eggs and avocados more often than Cheetos and frosted flakes. Eat plenty of fruits and vegetables. Get a variety of different wholesome, real foods and all the nutrients will stack up and—guess what—you'll meet your nutrient needs."[10]

Mangieri says that such a balanced diet for teens typically includes three meals plus two healthy snacks each day. The meals she recommends include foods such as eggs, whole grain toast, milk, and fruit for breakfast; a lunch of tuna salad on whole wheat bread, milk, fruit, and pretzels; and a supper of meat, vegetable, and potato. She suggests snacks like yogurt, granola, bran cereal, iron-fortified cereals, milk, bananas, berries, and nuts.

> "Get a variety of different wholesome, real foods and all the nutrients will stack up and— guess what—you'll meet your nutrient needs."[10]
>
> —Alissa Rumsey, dietitian

The Junk Food Scenario

No one is going to give up pizza, fast foods, or chocolate cake entirely, but experts recommend indulging in junk foods only occasionally. Many fast foods and take-out foods, as well as sweet treats and other snacks, are really junk foods. Junk foods are those that are very high in fats, salt, and sugars but very low in nutritional value. Canadian neuroscientist Amy Reichelt knows that junk foods are hard for teens to resist. She remembers, "Looking back, eating junk food was a huge part of my teenage life. I knew it wasn't nutritious, but damn—it's cheap, tasty and everywhere! When I was in high school, I often snuck out to a local Mac-Donald's or a donut shop. My weekends were spent socialising with friends hanging out at malls—gossiping over burgers, milkshakes, fries or pizza."[11]

Reichelt explains that it is natural for teens to crave rich, sweet, fatty foods and to have a hard time resisting them. It is all part of brain development. The emotional center of the brain matures before the prefrontal cortex, which means that negative emotions

Teens often crave rich, sweet, fatty foods that lack the nutrients necessary for normal physical and mental development. Experts recommend that such junk food be eaten only occasionally.

and stress can push teens to seek out the comfort that sweet and fatty foods provide. The trouble is that a regular diet of junk foods can have a major effect on mood and even mental health. This means that the junk food that is so tasty and comforting can actually cause more moodiness, unhappiness, and stress.

Eating a regular diet of junk food can create a vicious cycle of needing more and more of the food to feel good. Mental health may suffer, and brain development, along with the ability to perform academically, remember, and learn, may suffer, too. In addition, overeating of high-calorie junk foods can lead to weight gain and the risk of developing diabetes in the future. Some studies have shown that young people who eat at fast food restaurants more than twice a week double the chance of unwanted weight gain and the risk of future diabetes compared to those who frequent the restaurants less than once a week. And unwanted weight gain can make teens feel even more stressed and unhappy. Reichelt believes that teens have the right to know the facts about the effects of junk food on their health and their developing brains. She says, "If I'd been told that junk food could reduce my ability to study, I would probably have thought twice about eating a whole bag of Tim Bits [doughnut holes] while [studying] for exams!"[12]

A Word on Dieting

A healthy lifestyle may not include regularly overeating junk foods, but it does not mean dieting either. In general, weight-loss diets are not healthy for teens, because their nutritional needs are so high. Sometimes, weight-loss diets can even become dangerous and lead to eating disorders, such as anorexia and bulimia. Anorexia is a medical condition in which an individual is obsessed with losing weight, is often unable to eat, and becomes seriously ill. Bulimia is a condition in which an individual binge eats large amounts of food and then vomits or uses laxatives to undo the bingeing. For teens who are overweight, there are no quick fixes or shortcuts to getting healthy. Fad diets and skipping meals do

Defeating Acne

When actress and author Cameron Diaz was a teen, she suffered with an embarrassing and difficult problem. She remembers, "I used to have horrible acne—deep, boiling pimples—the kind that hurt so badly, I didn't want to leave my house." She also was thin and could eat anything she wanted without gaining weight, so she practically lived on fatty junk foods, never seeing a connection between her diet and her skin. She ate cheese burritos, french fries, onion rings, and double cheeseburgers. Finally, after trying everything else, Diaz gave up junk foods and began eating only whole, natural foods. Her acne disappeared, and she recalls that her energy surged. She says now, "I didn't realize all that fried, greasy, processed artificial crap was setting off a hormonal surge that sent my skin into crazy town!" Diaz became a believer in the benefits of good nutrition. Although she still indulges in unhealthy food sometimes, she remains committed to a mostly balanced, healthy diet today.

Quoted in Tamara Abraham, "'I Was the Poster Child for Being Both Skinny and Unhealthy': Cameron Diaz on How Her Teenage Love for Junk Food Caused Painful Acne," *Daily Mail* (London), January 9, 2014. www.dailymail.co.uk.

not work except in the short term. The weight loss cannot be maintained, health can deteriorate, and emotional problems may develop.

Instead, according to the website SafeTeens.org, the best diet means adopting a healthy lifestyle. The site advises, "The key is limiting how much unhealthy foods you eat. Eat more fruits and vegetables and eat fewer fatty meats like burgers. Cut back on fried food and candy. Replace soda and sports drinks with water. This does not mean you can never have a soda, it just means that having one daily is not healthy."[13]

Following a healthy diet is actually simple, but that does not mean it is necessarily easy. People have to make a conscious lifestyle choice to stick with wholesome foods.

CHAPTER TWO

Grocery Shopping and Cooking

Of necessity, people who want to eat a healthy diet will eventually find themselves buying foods and preparing meals. If you live at home with parents who provide healthy meals, that's great, but this might not be the case for everyone. If you are heading off to college, you may not always be able to afford or take advantage of the cafeteria meal plans. And if you are getting ready to move to a place of your own, there is no time to waste. Buying groceries and cooking meals is neither as time consuming nor as difficult as many people think.

Braving the Grocery Store

Grocery shopping can be intimidating for first-timers. As a college student at American University, Faith Branch, commented, "Being an adult is difficult, especially when you are super lazy—and grocery shopping can be a real struggle without your parents helping you navigate the store and paying for everything at the end." Branch offers some tips about how to grocery shop "like an adult." She suggests strategies such as always making a grocery list so that you don't overspend, remembering to stop and get a cart because you will undoubtedly need it, choosing generic brands rather than brand names to save money, and visiting the

Finding nutritious food at the grocery store is an important skill that requires some thought and planning.

frozen food aisle last so that your frozen foods don't melt before you finish shopping. She also warns, "It's really easy to get lost in the store when grocery shopping. So when I'm trying to get in and out without buying too much junk food, I walk along the edges of the store first. The essentials can usually be found here and it easier to see what is in each aisle without actually going down the aisle."[14]

Shopping the perimeter of the grocery store is recommended by many nutrition experts and dietitians. The reasoning behind this strategy is simple. Health and nutrition educator Sara Ipatenco explains, "In many grocery stores, the inner aisles are stocked with sugary, fatty and high-calorie snacks, packaged goods and frozen dinners. The outer areas of the store usually stock fresh produce, lean meats and low-fat dairy foods."[15] Poultry, fish and other seafood, as well as the bakery and bread sections are also generally located around the perimeter.

Dietitian Jill Castle, however, points out that the center aisles of grocery stores stock healthy, nutritious foods, too, and many non-perishable foods can be found there if you shop wisely. "Nuts and seeds and dried fruits, healthier oils, beans, whole grain pastas, brown rice," she says. "There are lots of good finds in the aisles." Because everyone knows that snacks are sometimes irresistible, Castle also explains that bothering to read ingredients is worth-while if you are going to buy some treats along with healthy foods. She adds, "I advise teens to look at the first three ingredients. You want to be able to identify what's in it, and you want to be able to pronounce it. If you look at a bag of Lay's potato chips, the ingredients are potatoes, salt, oil. If you pick up a bag of cheesy Doritos, you see a lot of chemicals you can't pronounce."[16]

Buying Fresh

Even shopping grocery store perimeters is not without pitfalls. Fresh fruits and vegetables, dairy products, meat and fish, and even bakery goods are not full of preservatives and therefore can spoil or go bad. You have to check your foods before you buy. Fruits and vegetables should be firm, have good color, and appear fresh. Dairy and meat products have expiration dates that let customers estimate how long the foods will last once brought home. Expiration dates refer to food quality rather than safety when it comes to food. They are general guidelines and do not have to be followed strictly. For instance, an expiration date on a carton of eggs (sometimes a "Sell by" date) suggests the eggs will last another three or four weeks in your home refrigerator if bought before that date. "Use

> "In many grocery stores, the inner aisles are stocked with sugary, fatty and high-calorie snacks, packaged goods and frozen dinners. The outer areas of the store usually stock fresh produce, lean meats and low-fat dairy foods."[15]
>
> —Sara Ipatenco, health and nutrition educator

Save Money and Cook!

As a student at Virginia Commonwealth University, Meagan Conley quickly learned that cooking her own meals saved money. At her college, Conley explains, each swipe of her meal card is supposed to equal a twelve-dollar meal. That meant that if she got a bowl of oatmeal and a waffle for breakfast, for instance, she had just spent twelve dollars for very little food. So, Conley says,

> What I do for breakfast is buy a bulk box of oatmeal and have a bowl of that every morning. One 42 oz. box of Old-fashioned Quaker Oatmeal from Target costs $4.19, which can make at least 20 bowls of oatmeal. That would mean each of those breakfasts cost a mere 20 cents. Now, I do like to add other foods into my oatmeal, like blueberries when they are in season and chia and flax seeds to benefit my body, which I did not calculate into the meal price. But for a basic breakfast to get your day started that costs 20 cents, making your own meal seems much cheaper than using a dining plan. . . . Ditch the meal plan and stick to cooking. It can be much cheaper if you know what you are doing!

Meagan Conley, "How Cooking Can Be Cheaper than Getting a Meal Plan," Her Campus Media, November 17, 2017. www.hercampus.com.

by" dates indicate when to eat the product for peak quality. Even after that date, the food may still be fine if it was kept refrigerated. However, a bag of salad mix, for instance, may become wilted and appear unappetizing if saved much past the "Use by" date.

Often, the best way to check the quality of food is to look at it and smell it, not to go by the expiration date. Keep in mind that foods can go bad even on a store shelf. Branch remembers,

> Once while I was grocery shopping I picked up cheese that was already moldy and the expiration date wasn't until the next month. This also goes for eggs because some-

times a few of the eggs in the carton are already cracked and they are of no use pre-opened. Just to be safe, always check to make sure that what you pick up isn't spoiled.[17]

The same goes for fruits and vegetables. Turn over the carton of berries and look to be sure no mold is visible. Examine the carton of fresh mushrooms to determine if any liquid is oozing out. A brief look is all that is needed to ensure what you buy is fresh.

A Cooking Adventure

Once all your healthy, fresh groceries are home, it is time to figure out what to do with them, and many times that means getting into the kitchen and cooking. Although you may need to buy a few basics such as a toaster, a frying pan or skillet, and a sharp knife to get started, you do not even need a cookbook to learn to cook. Nowadays, thousands of recipes are available on the Internet, and some websites, such as Spoon University, are dedicated to college students and others who want advice and simple, healthy recipes. One contributor writing for Spoon University, for instance, describes how she cooked for the first time in her parents' kitchen without their help. She was planning to go to college in a few months at a college without a student meal plan, so she felt like she had to try. She explains, "I always had a fascination with cooking, but never ventured into the kitchen myself to cook because I was always scared of setting my house on fire or burning the food."[18]

> "Just to be safe, always check to make sure that what you pick up isn't spoiled."[17]
>
> —Faith Branch, college student

Her first step was to search the Internet for a recipe that seemed appealing. She searched Google for "quick and healthy recipes in under 20 minutes" and found hundreds of recipes, but she did not settle for a particularly easy one. She chose one titled "honey garlic shrimp" because she knew she would like it. After a grocery shopping trip to buy all the ingredients, she set to work.

She mixed ingredients to make the sauce, marinated the shrimp for an hour in the refrigerator, and then cooked shrimp and sauce in a pan. She also cooked brown rice and broccoli in two separate saucepans of boiling water on top of the stove. When everything was done, she was pleasantly surprised to discover that the meal was tasty. She remembers:

> I enjoyed cooking a lot more than I thought I would by the time I was finished. . . . I liked how I was able to make food that I wanted and see a finished product by the time I was finished. Even though I have relatively bad anxiety about cooking and everything else, I was still able to accomplish this task successfully. . . . I would highly recommend trying to get into the kitchen and see if you like it because you never know what will happen unless you try![19]

Preparing a meal from fresh, healthy ingredients can be an enjoyable and satisfying experience.

Recipes for College Students

Michael, a student at the Massachusetts Institute of Technology, decided to try cooking to save money and be able to eat tastier, healthier food than he could on the student meal plan. He had never cooked in his life, but he easily figured it out. To begin, he bought himself a chef's pan, a saucepan, a toaster, a chef's knife, a paring knife, and a spatula. With just those few kitchen items, he cooks almost anything he wants. Michael likes chicken, steaks, pork, and shrimp and builds his dinners around these protein foods, but he enjoys vegetables like onions, mushrooms, tomatoes, bell peppers, and spinach, too. For breakfast, he has discovered that a veggie omelet is simple and takes only about seven minutes to cook. He cooks whatever vegetables he has on hand, such as mushrooms, spinach leaves, and chopped onions and peppers, in olive oil in his chef's pan for a couple of minutes. Then he adds eggs and scrambles them right in the pan for another minute. He says that this omelet is so easy that even a groggy, half-asleep student can do it.

For dinner, Michael might cook steak in his chef's pan, too. He recommends, "For when you want to be a little fancy, get a New York strip steak (by the way—the meal plan's so expensive that you could cook a NY strip steak every night and still save money. Just sayin'.)." Or he might have shrimp with pasta. The shrimp is cooked in his trusty chef's pan, and the pasta goes into boiling water in his saucepan. (Add just a little vegetable oil to the water and the pasta won't stick to the pan.) Michael explains about his choice of pasta, "For carbs, I usually get pasta because it's fast and easy and I like Italian food. Rice takes longer and is harder to get right on the stovetop."[20]

Food Handling Safety

Because cooking has to include some appreciation of safe food handling, Michael also offers some meat safety tips. He says, "The USDA [US Department of Agriculture] recommends cooking chicken to 165°F, eggs and ground meat to 160°F, beef and pork

Iodized Salt

When you are shopping for kitchen staples, it is a good idea to buy iodized salt. Iodine is a trace element found in the soil, but in large parts of the world that are far from the oceans, the soil may be deficient in iodine. Severe iodine deficiency can cause goiters (swelling of the neck where the thyroid gland is); hypothyroidism (a disease characterized by weight gain, depression, tiredness, coldness, and dry skin); and birth defects in babies. While serious iodine deficiency is rare in the developed world, some studies have found that perhaps 40 percent of Americans are borderline deficient. Perhaps they eat at restaurants that do not use iodized salt; perhaps they are following a restrictive diet, such as veganism or a paleo diet; perhaps they are extremely reducing salt in the diet. Too much salt may be unhealthy, but salt with added iodine is a safe way to prevent iodine deficiency. Choosing iodized salt in the grocery store is a simple way to ensure enough iodine in your diet without ever having to think about it.

to 145°F. This, of course, means very little to the starving student without a food thermometer. As a rule of thumb: cook chicken and ground meat until it's cooked through. Cook pork until there's a touch of pink left. Cook steak however rare you want it."[21]

When cooking, a few basic safety tips are important. The USDA suggests three other tips for cooking meals safely: Keep hands and preparation surfaces clean. Keep raw meat, fish, and their juices separate from other foods. (In other words, don't slice the tomatoes for your salad on the same plate that you used to cut your chicken unless you first washed the plate thoroughly.) Refrigerate any leftovers promptly so that bacteria have no chance to grow. With just a little knowledge and experience, anyone can cook healthy and tasty meals that are safe to eat.

CHAPTER THREE

Physical Activity

The Centers for Disease Control and Prevention (CDC) states that children and adolescents need regular physical activity in order to promote health and well-being throughout their lifetime. The benefits of physical activity during the teen years are well established. The CDC explains:

> Regular physical activity can help children and adolescents improve cardiorespiratory [heart and lung] fitness, build strong bones and muscles, control weight, reduce symptoms of anxiety and depression, and reduce the risk of developing health conditions such as:
> * Heart disease.
> * Cancer.
> * Type 2 diabetes.
> * High blood pressure.
> * Osteoporosis.
> * Obesity.[22]

Inactivity and Teens

The effects of inactivity or a sedentary lifestyle include an increased risk for unhealthy conditions, both in the present and in the future. Energy imbalance, for example, can have an immediate effect on a teen's health. Energy imbalance means using less energy than

Inactivity and a sedentary lifestyle can lead to unhealthy conditions such as unwanted weight gain and even obesity.

one takes in via calories. The result can be unwanted weight gain and even obesity. About 30 percent of kids ages two to nineteen are either overweight or obese, and about 70 percent of obese young people already have at least one risk factor for developing heart disease, such as high cholesterol levels, atherosclerosis, high blood pressure, or insulin resistance. Atherosclerosis is a condition in which plaque (made up of hardened fats and other substances) builds up inside the arteries. Insulin resistance refers to the body's impaired ability to use the hormone insulin to transport glucose (sugars) to body cells for energy. Insulin resistance can eventually lead to diabetes.

Of course, diet has a considerable impact on weight, but according to the CDC, inactivity and energy imbalance play a major role, too. Increasing energy output through exercise helps correct the imbalance and prevent weight gain. Diseases such as cancer, osteoporosis, or heart disease may not affect an overweight, inactive teen for decades, but teens do develop some diseases at young ages. Some fifty-three hundred people ages ten to nineteen already have the kind of diabetes related to lifestyle. About 4 percent of people ages twelve to nineteen have high blood pressure. Exercise can dramatically turn these diseases around. And even a teen who shows no signs of disease can feel healthier and happier with the right amount of activity.

According to the CDC, teens should get about one hour of physical activity each day in order to be healthy. Few teens, however, meet this goal. The CDC reports, "Only 27.1% of high school students participate in at least 60 minutes per day of physical activity on all 7 days of the week."[23] Another study estimates that only 25 percent of people ages twelve to twenty-one engage in even light physical activity every day.

For college students, says a research team led by Jesse Calestine of Pennsylvania State University, there is a decrease in physical activity and an increase in sedentary behavior. In their study of physical fitness and academic workload, Calestine and her colleagues found that heavier academic workloads and increased study time often meant decreased physical activity in college students. The researchers say, "During college years, there are a number of personal habits that have the potential to impact health behaviors, including time management, academic activities, leisure activities and social media use."[24] In other words, students who want to live a healthy lifestyle have to choose a schedule for themselves that balances work, leisure time, and physical activity.

> "Only 27.1% of high school students participate in at least 60 minutes per day of physical activity on all 7 days of the week."[23]
>
> —The CDC

How to Get Active

Regular exercise helps people become successful students by increasing memory and ability to focus, improving mood, lowering tension and stress levels, and increasing energy. The Student

Health and Counseling Services at the University of California, Davis, says, "Staying physically active as a college student can be hard, but we have some strategies and tips to help you stay active now and down the road."[25] The group's tips are useful for teens of any age. First, they recommend, schedule time for physical activity, just as you have to do for classes, study time, and social activities. Then find a way to make the activity more enjoyable by making it social. Running, walking, or a workout at the gym is more fun with a friend, and you can encourage each other to stick with the routine. Schedule time for a casual game of softball, soccer, or Frisbee with a group of friends whenever possible. And choose an activity you enjoy and one that works best for you so that you will look forward to it and want to do it.

Even if a rigid exercise routine does not fit into your life or match your personality, you can be active. Several University of

Heart Healthy

When Austin Frampton was fourteen years old, he joined the CrossFit gym that his older brother owns. Frampton enjoyed both the comradeship with his brother and the workout program his brother set up for him. When he first started, Frampton was unable to do even one push-up or pull-up. A year later and attending the gym several times a week, the now fifteen-year-old could manage twenty-six push-ups and fifteen pull-ups. That was when Frampton surprised his doctor. Frampton has Down syndrome and a hole in his heart, a defect that is common for people with Down syndrome. The doctor was monitoring Frampton regularly, in order to determine when his health would require surgery to repair the heart defect. Frampton became so healthy and fit, however, that the doctor considered surgery unnecessary. The repair may be needed in the future, but at age eighteen, Frampton was a high school senior, a huge supporter of his high school basketball team, and still healthy, active, and physically fit.

Companionship makes a workout such as jogging more enjoyable, which encourages sticking to an exercise routine.

California, Davis, students offer many different ideas for how they stay physically fit at college. The students suggest:

- Take the stairs
- Play on the jungle gym
- Sign up for an exercise class
- Walk to class
- Walk during lunch in the arboretum
- Jumping jacks whenever possible
- Wake up an hour early every morning
- Track my steps
- Dance away the stress
- 10 minutes of yoga every morning.[26]

Making It Fun

Sometimes finding an activity that is pleasurable can be difficult, so flexibility and a willingness to reassess choices are important.

Diabetes Does Not Win

Jaime Rangel was fourteen years old when he was diagnosed with type 2 diabetes. This kind of diabetes occurs when the body does not make enough insulin or cannot properly use the insulin it makes. Insulin is the key that opens the body's cells so that glucose can get into and feed the cells. In type 2 diabetes, the glucose remains in the blood, and blood sugar levels rise. Rangel was scared by his diabetes diagnosis. He had seen his mother and several relatives suffer with diabetes. His doctor told him to lose weight and exercise. A friend gave him a bike, and he began riding. He loved it, and soon he was riding throughout his city of Los Angeles. He even rode to the beach, 20 miles (32 km) away from home. After one year, Rangel's glucose levels were normal. He remembers, "Biking changed my life. I lost a lot of weight." He persuaded his family to begin to ride bikes with him, and their diabetes vastly improved, too. The exercise had changed their bodies' sensitivity to insulin and reversed their diabetes. Today Rangel works with other city youth to encourage them to be active and healthy through cycling.

Quoted in Farida Jhabvala Romero, "Cyclist Teaches Kids to Use Fun to Prevent Type 2 Diabetes," National Public Radio, May 3, 2016. www.npr.org.

When Tina Ma, for example, was a high school freshman, she wanted to play volleyball. She tried out for her school's junior varsity (JV) team with enthusiasm and high hopes, but she immediately felt uncomfortable. She explains,

> I was in a room of girls who had played years of club volleyball and had a lot of experience. They had known each other since kindergarten (I was new). I struggled with unfamiliar drills (I had never played club volleyball) and making friends (my lack of skill did not contribute to my confidence level).[27]

Tina wanted to succeed, but she felt awkward and left out. She just did not belong and was unhappy. She ended up being kicked off the team, but instead of giving up, she looked around for another sport she could do. She decided to try water polo and remembers:

> I immediately fit in. The other girls were warm, supportive and not annoyed by my technical mistakes. The team was new, and most participants were at my skill level. We could laugh at our own mistakes. I felt that I truly belonged in this aquatic environment. I felt infinitely more comfortable at the pool with my new Varsity Water Polo teammates than at the gym with the JV Volleyball team.[28]

Tina's advice to others is always to be willing to seek out new people and new activities to try.

Some people dislike team sports, but that doesn't mean they cannot find fun activities. The Canadian Society for Exercise Physiology says, "Every step counts!"[29] and has developed a list of activities for teens to choose from. They range from simple things, such as taking the dog for a walk, dancing to music in your living room, bike riding, running, or raking leaves at home to interesting after-school classes like hip-hop, indoor rock climbing, and yoga. The society also suggests just having fun with swimming, skating, skateboarding, skiing, sledding, or snowboarding.

Varied Activity Opportunities

Despite the usual recommendations to combine physical activities with social interactions, some people do not want to exercise around others. Other people may not feel they have the time to schedule regular exercise with their friends or on a team. The National Institute of Diabetes and Digestive and Kidney Diseases (NIDDK) urges teens to be physically active and take responsibility for their own health, whether individually or in a group. It recommends that most of the daily hour of activity be aerobic exercise, but if that is not possible, aerobics should be included at least three times a week. Aerobic exercise, also known as "cardio," increases breathing and heart rates and keeps the heart, lungs, and circulatory system healthy. Examples of aerobic exercise that can be done alone include running, biking, and dancing.

Anaerobic or resistance exercise such as lifting weights, on the other hand, promotes muscle strength and endurance. Both kinds of exercise are important and increase energy output, but even light activity, such as a walk along a flat path, is of benefit and counts as exercise.

The NIDDK also emphasizes, "You don't have to do your 60 minutes a day all at once to benefit from your activity."[30]

Neither does every activity have to be vigorous. For instance, the NIDDK explains that just cleaning your room or taking out the trash can be part of regular activity and counts as moving and getting exercise. Since exercise minutes add up, a ten-minute walk to a friend's house plus the ten-minute walk back home again plus perhaps ten minutes of running around with the dog in the backyard equals half the exercise one needs in a day. Add thirty minutes of playing basketball (an aerobic activity) and you have the one hour of exercise for that day.

Even in Your Own Backyard

As a matter of fact, the backyard can become an excellent place to get fit. Australian student Mele Osai was too ashamed of herself to exercise in public. She was fourteen years old, lived a sedentary lifestyle, and weighed 297 pounds (135 kg). One day she was walking home from school and became so exhausted and out of breath that she had to sit down and rest. Suddenly, she realized that something had to change. Her doctor told her that she was on the path to developing diabetes, as well. Osai wanted to lose weight and radically changed her diet to healthy foods, but exercise was a problem. She remembers, "When you're that big, you feel . . . a bit of an outcast. I found it hard to fit in to social situations . . . playing sport was hard because my weight held me back."[31] So she set up a kind of exercise gym in her own backyard, complete with weights, where she could work out in private.

Over the next two years, Osai lost 143 pounds (65 kg) and fell in love with weight training. At age sixteen, she had the confidence to join a gym, not to lose any more weight but for fun, toning, and strengthening. She takes long daily walks, too, and plans to study fitness in college. Osai is healthy and happy and wants other teens to know that there is always a way to choose physical fitness and an active, healthy lifestyle.

CHAPTER FOUR

Sleep

The National Sleep Foundation is a nonprofit organization dedicated to public understanding and research into the importance of sleep. The organization says, "Sleep is vital to your well-being, as important as the air you breathe, the water you drink and the food you eat. It can even help you to eat better and manage the stress of being a teen."[32] Teens need eight to ten hours of sleep each night, yet research shows that only 15 percent of teens get at last eight and a half hours of sleep regularly.

The Big Sleep Problem

Teens have a particular biological reason for having trouble getting enough sleep. At puberty their biological clocks begin to change. Their sleep-wake cycles shift from the patterns of childhood and remain this way until they are about twenty years old. The brain hormones that control sleepiness, particularly melatonin, are released later at night. The delay in sleepiness is about two hours compared to children or adults. This change gradually causes teens to have trouble falling asleep early and to naturally stay wakeful later and later. A teen's natural biological clock keeps him or her awake until about eleven o'clock at night. That same cycle keeps sleep hormones high early in the morning, so teens have as much trouble waking up at 6:30 a.m. to get ready for school as adults would have beginning their day at 4:30 a.m. The vast majority of teens around the world, adjusting to adult and societal schedules (like school start times), are chronically sleep deprived and getting an average of only seven hours of nightly sleep. For many it is like living with constant jet lag.

For years sleep experts have advocated for later school starting times for teens, citing studies that show increased alertness, elevated moods, and better academic performance in teens who start classes even thirty minutes later in the day. However, few schools have made the change. In large part that means it is up to teens themselves to figure out ways to get enough sleep. It matters because the effects of long-term sleep deprivation are so dramatic.

> "Sleep is vital to your well-being, as important as the air you breathe, the water you drink and the food you eat."[32]
>
> —The National Sleep Foundation

The Effects of Sleep Deprivation

Lack of sleep can have as big an effect on healthy weight as food and exercise do. One consequence of inadequate sleep is a craving for sweets and fatty fried foods. This occurs, in part, because these junk foods give quick energy boosts to people who feel tired and also because lack of sleep increases the production of a hormone that causes hunger. Professor Lauren Hale and a research team conducted a study of more than thirteen thousand teens and discovered that food choices were directly related to hours of nightly sleep, especially in teens sleeping fewer than seven hours a night. Hale reports, "Not only do sleepy teens on average eat more food that's bad for them, they also eat less food that is good for them."[33] On average, chronically sleepy teens ate more fast food and fewer fruits and vegetables than teens sleeping more than eight hours a night. Another study at the University of Warwick in England, completed in 2018, found evidence that teens who are regularly sleep deprived gain more weight as they grow older and are 58 percent more likely to become overweight.

Unhealthy food choices and weight gain, however, are not the only consequences of sleep deprivation. Researchers have

Lack of proper sleep can interfere with a teenager's ability to concentrate, problem solve, and remember information.

discovered that chronic deprivation contributes to acne and skin breakouts in teens. It also has a major effect on mood and mental health. One study found that sleep-deprived teens are four times more likely to become depressed than teens getting enough sleep. Other studies have discovered increased irritability, aggression, anxiety, and low self-esteem in chronically sleep-deprived teens. A sleepy student's academic performance can suffer, too. Not getting enough sleep can decrease the ability to concentrate, problem solve, and remember. Each teen is different, and no one knows in what ways sleep deprivation will affect an individual, but scientists do know that everyone experiences negative consequences when they don't get enough sleep.

Sleep expert Mary A. Carskadon explains that many teens are very good at hiding their sleepiness, even from themselves. She says,

Teens may be driven to [do] things that can wake them up simply because they'll fall asleep if they do not. So we see caffeine, late-night Internet, chat rooms, IM'ing, cramming in activity after activity as a means to keep awake and necessitating more of the same to stay awake in the face of declining sleep. . . . These patterns can disguise the extent of their sleep deficit for many teens.[34]

Nevertheless, Carskadon asserts, signs of sleep deprivation show up in chronically exhausted teens in disturbing ways. She continues:

> Thus, we see the teenager who falls asleep driving home late at night; in another teen, the problem emerges with titanic struggles to wake up in the morning, often failing and resulting in late or missed school; another may simply feel sad and moody and blue, lacking initiative or motivation; in other teens, grades begin to suffer as the teen struggles to keep awake during class and while doing homework; another may turn to heavier drugs to get some positive and

Let Go and Go to Sleep

As a junior at Indiana University, Kelly Morgan found helpful advice for the times that her worries kept her from falling asleep after she went to bed at night. The strategy was given to her by an advanced practice nurse at a sleep center: When you cannot fall asleep because you are thinking about problems, get out of bed and write each worry on a note card. On the back of each card, write down what you will do about it. Morgan explains further, "If you don't know the answer, then write that you can't do anything about the problem until the following day. The kindergarten teacher who told you to journal your feelings actually made a good point. Seeing our worries on paper might actually help us realize how ridiculous and worrisome humans act." It is a simple tip that might help anyone relax and get a good night's sleep.

Kelly Morgan, "Survival Tips for the Sleep-Deprived College Student," *College Magazine*, December 28, 2015. www.collegemagazine.com.

arousing sensations; many just struggle along in a kind of haze, never knowing how to feel or do their best.[35]

Resolving Sleep Issues

If you know that you are not getting enough sleep, how can you make sleep a priority in your life? Often the answer is not easy, but there are solutions. A top suggestion offered by sleep experts is to try to adjust your body's biological clock. It takes time, but even being able to fall asleep a half hour earlier has an appreciable benefit. The body's clock is controlled by a part of the brain in the hypothalamus that responds to light entering the eye. When it is dark, the brain signals the release of sleep hormones, such as melatonin, that make people feel sleepy. When it is light, the signals received indicate that it is time to be awake. Practically speaking, this means that dimming the lights as your chosen bedtime

Avoiding screen time for one to three hours before going to bed makes it easier to fall asleep and get a good night's rest.

approaches helps you begin to get sleepy. Over a six-week period, try going to bed ten minutes earlier each week to reset your clock. Then, in the morning, it helps to get into bright light as soon as possible in order to stimulate wakefulness. Sleep expert Dr. Heidi Moawad recommends avoiding too much light all evening as a way of avoiding suppressing the release of melatonin in teens. She reports that teens are particularly sensitive to light, and that is one reason they have trouble going to sleep before 11:00 p.m.

Unfortunately, the brain does not just respond to light from the sun and electric lights. It also responds to light from screens— televisions, tablets, smartphones, and computer gaming systems. One study found that teens who avoid screen time for one hour before going to bed gain an extra twenty-one minutes of sleep nightly by increasing the release of melatonin earlier in the evening. Almost all sleep experts suggest no screen time for one to three hours before you want to be able to go to sleep.

Blue Light Blues

The wavelength of light that is most powerful in suppressing melatonin is blue light, mostly from the sun but also from screens. This means that even if you turn off all the lights in your room, using a phone or computer at night will prevent you from getting sleepy. The National Sleep Foundation recognizes that it is not always possible to avoid screen time at night. Busy students may need to do homework or research a paper. Others may only have time to socialize with friends on screens at night. So the organization says that

> it helps to dim the brightness on the screen. Or, you can in-
> stall an app that automatically warms up the colors on the
> screen—away from blues and toward reds and yellows—
> at sunset. Also, avoid using energy-efficient (blue) bulbs in
> nightlights in bedrooms and bathrooms; opt for dim red
> lights instead because red light has a higher wavelength
> and does not suppress the release of melatonin.[36]

Sleep Disorders

Although less common than in adults, sleep disorders can leave teens sleep deprived. Sleep disorders are conditions like chronic insomnia, restless legs syndrome, and sleep apnea that prevent people from getting restful, restorative sleep. Sleep apnea, for instance, is a condition resulting from an obstructed airway. People with sleep apnea have repeated episodes in which breathing stops for brief periods while they are asleep. Symptoms include loud snoring, snorting or gasping during the night, chronic sleepiness and tiredness during the day, and waking in the morning with headaches or a sore throat. People with sleep apnea have disrupted sleep and never get the rest they need. Once diagnosed by a doctor, the problem and its cause can be addressed. Some people may need to have tonsils and adenoids removed if these tissues obstruct the airway when lying down. Others may need to lose weight. Still others wear a dental appliance from their dentist to keep the airway open. Some use continuous positive airway pressure, or CPAP, machines at night that use forced air pressure to open the airway. The important thing about sleep disorders is to know they are treatable and to seek medical help.

Some scientists recommend the use of blue-light-blocking glasses. These glasses block blue light during screen time at night. In one 2015 Swiss study, a group of teen males wore blue-light-blocking glasses every evening for two weeks while working on computers. An equal number of teens wore regular clear glasses, and both groups were compared. At the end of the study, the researchers determined that, compared to the clear glasses, the blue-light-blocking glasses resulted in significantly decreased melatonin suppression in the study subjects. The teens who used the blue-light-blocking glasses also reported that they felt less alert and wakeful at bedtime.

Shawn A. Clark, a college student with his own website, agrees about the value of blue-light-blocking glasses, on the basis of his own experience. He says that his nightly extensive screen time for college work was ruining his ability to fall asleep. Using the glasses made all the difference for him. He explains,

> Blue light blocking glasses saved me from losing hours of sleep and improved my academic performance. I hated coding assignments because I had to stare at the screen for hours some nights to code and debug. It was difficult to fall asleep those days, but not anymore.[37]

He recommends the glasses for other college students coping with the same issue.

More Helpful Tips

For college students, roommates, dorm life, and academic demands can make getting enough sleep seem almost impossible. Students themselves recommend establishing a regular, soothing nighttime routine, bringing your favorite pillow to college, avoiding caffeine and alcohol after 4:00 p.m., exercising during the day (but at least three hours before bedtime), and avoiding a heavy meal before bed. Jennie Miremadi, a nutritionist and college wellness expert, adds, "If you live on a noisy dorm floor, get some earplugs or purchase a white noise machine to help block out the noise."[38]

"Remember, *any sleep* is better than *no sleep.*"[39]

—Maryellen Fitzgerald-Bord, college student

Preventing sleep deprivation is critical to an overall healthy lifestyle. College student Maryellen Fitzgerald-Bord recommends catnaps during the day for people who just can't get enough sleep at night. She advises, "Remember, *any sleep* is better than *no sleep.*"[39] Experts recommend early afternoon naps, too, for overtired teens, and some suggest that sleeping later on weekends does help people catch up on sleep. No matter what your situation, brainstorm ways to get your daily quota of sleep because your body and brain desperately need it for health, growth, and mental well-being.

CHAPTER FIVE

Social and Psychological Health

The National Longitudinal Study of Adolescent to Adult Health (abbreviated as Add Health) is a long-term study, begun in 1994, of more than twenty thousand teens ages twelve to seventeen. The goal is to learn how adolescent social environments and behaviors affect them now and in the future. The data is used by researchers around the world to learn more about the social, economic, psychological, and physical well-being of teens. Over the years, researchers have discovered a great many factors that determine social, psychological, and even physical health.

Be Very Social!

Kathleen Mullan Harris of the University of North Carolina, Chapel Hill, and director of the Add Health study, reports that social bonds are critical to teen health. She says that Add Health data demonstrates that during the teen years, close, supportive, and varied social relationships are important determinants of physical health. She explains, "In adolescence, social isolation is equivalent to the effects of getting no exercise." As the researchers looked at connections of teens with friends, family, acquaintances, and community, they examined measures of stress, such as blood pressure, unhealthy weight, and signs of inflammation in body organs. Harris says the fewer social connections people had, the

Research indicates that close, supportive, and varied social relationships have a positive effect on physical health.

worse off they were physically. She continues, "With each additional social connection that you have, you get an added beneficial effect for your health. The more, the better."[40] And as teens grow older (some of the original participants are now in their forties), these early social connections reduce the risk of illness or death by 50 percent. Harris urges all teens to participate in social groups and leisure activities with others as much as they can.

The ways in which social connections may influence health are probably many. Having a support system lowers stress and helps decrease its effects on the body. When people can talk out their troubles with an understanding friend or family member, they feel better. When they have the distractions of social activities, they are less likely to dwell on difficulties and worries. Harris speculates that friends and family help

> "With each additional social connection that you have, you get an added beneficial effect for your health. The more, the better."[40]
>
> —Kathleen Mullan Harris, director of the Add Health study

Finding a Happy Place

As a high school senior in 2016, Melissa Casey was overwhelmed with stress. Then she found a place where she could unwind, relax, and let go of her worries. Casey believes everyone needs to find a "happy place" for peace of mind and mental health. A happy place can be anything or anywhere. It can be the beach, a sports arena, the gym, or the library, but for Casey it was an indoor cycling center called SoulCycle. There, in a candlelit room with music playing, she can ride an indoor bicycle in a community of like-minded people. Casey says:

> I have made so many memories throughout the three years I have been going to SoulCycle. Being there puts me at such ease and gives me a stress relief once or twice a week. . . . It does not matter what fitness level you are or the experience you have with cycling. It gives people a chance to make new friendships, relationships and memories that will continue to grow from trying something new.

She urges everyone to be open to new things and try new experiences in order to find their happy place.

Melissa Casey, "A Happy Place; How to Find One and How It Benefits You," Loquitur, February 18, 2019. www.theloquitur.com.

teens in practical ways, too. For instance, a supportive parent is likely to urge a teen to eat his or her vegetables. A caring boyfriend might push his girlfriend to get more sleep. In some circumstances friends and family might remind young people to be sure to take their prescribed medicine or encourage them to go to the doctor to check out a medical issue. Supportive relationships might also be factors in discouraging people from experimenting with unhealthy habits, such as driving recklessly or using drugs or alcohol.

Not all friendship groups, however, are necessarily beneficial. Using the data collected by Add Health, other researchers at the University of Warwick in the United Kingdom discovered that moods and symptoms of depression, such as feelings of help-lessness and loss of interest in life, can spread across groups of friends. In other words, hanging around with people who are frequently in a bad mood or feeling low can make you feel moody and low, too. The frequency of those feelings increases with an individual's contacts with low mood friends. Fortunately, the researchers found the reverse to be true, as well. Teens whose friends mostly experience positive moods feel more positive themselves. But feelings are not the only factors influenced by friends and their emotions. According to the Golden Goose Award, which annually recognizes especially significant benefits of federally funded research, Add Health data yielded some surprising connections between friends and physical health. The Golden Goose Award website reports, "Using Add Health data, researchers have discovered that unhealthy conditions like obesity can actually spread among friend groups in ways analogous to contagious viruses."[41]

Friends are critically important to health, but the kinds of friendship matter. It's important for teens who want to help a friend to be aware of the possibilities of contagion, whether of mood or diet. Knowing that unhealthy feelings and behaviors can be contagious will help prevent you from falling into the same unhealthy patterns as your friend.

Focus on Friendships

The Add Health data does not mean that you have to be popular to have a healthy lifestyle. It does not mean that you are doomed if you don't have a loving family. It does mean, however, that you cannot sit alone in your room and never connect with anyone. You have to get out and interact with people. Some people find these connections through churches, school or community clubs, or volunteer work. Others engage in sports or leisure activities that involve other people. Harlan Cohen is an author who has talked to hundreds of college students throughout the country about how hard it can be to avoid isolation and to make new friends when starting college. He recommends, "Whenever you go to new places on campus, be open to making new friends—I like to call them temporary friends—who hold a place until they become permanent, or at least good or trustworthy, friends." He says that it takes patience and a willingness to take some risks but that just getting out and about is worth it. He suggests, for instance, "Eat outside, or study outside, just go for a walk outside, or even sit and look at your phone outside! People will be like, 'Hey, hi, I know you!' Or, if you don't know anyone, you'll be like, 'Oh that person's starting to look familiar.'"[42] Such small steps can lead to big friendships eventually.

Recent college graduate Ransom Patterson has written a complete guide to making friends at college. He has put together some good advice, especially for people who are introverts like he is and find socializing difficult. He insists that while you can't force friendship, you can actively seek it out. He says that you have to do things in order to meet people, and he suggests attending interesting campus events such as music festivals, protests, or marathons for charity or seeking out campus organizations and clubs that match your interests. He reminds students that classes, especially those with labs or group projects, provide opportunities to begin to talk to someone and that dorm life offers great chances to meet people, even if it is only saying hello to the person passing you in the hall.

> "At the end of the day, the best advice I can give for making friends is to make it a priority."[43]
>
> —Ransom Patterson, author and recent college graduate

Campus jobs and internships are also easy avenues for meeting and talking to new people. Once you have made a friend, says Patterson, it is relatively simple to maintain the friendship. He explains, "Just keep in touch and do things together regularly." Then, he advises, be open to branching out and expanding your circle of friends with new classes, new activities, and new interests. He concludes, "At the end of the day, the best advice I can give for making friends is to make it a priority. Once you've achieved that mindset shift, your job is to get out there and make it happen."[43]

Make Mental Health a Priority

For some people at some times in their lives, following advice about social health is not easy. Psychological wellness is a big part of being able to make social connections, and yet one in five teens and one in three freshman college students have trouble with mental health at some point, whether with anxiety, depression, or general stress. According to the Canadian website Teen Talk:

> Mental health is about the quality of our life and being able to find balance between the many parts of our lives— family, school, social life, relationships, activities, spiritual beliefs, and so on. It's almost impossible to have perfect mental health. Life is full of ups and downs, and everyone will face difficult and stressful situations. The cool thing is that we can all work at improving our mental health.[44]

Seeking help is important when dealing with stress, anxiety, or depression.

Psychologist Sherry Benton recommends four things that students can do to maintain and improve their mental health. Although she specifically refers to college students, most of her advice is suitable for all teens. First, she says, don't self-medicate with alcohol or drugs. Many teens assume that everyone else is normally using drinking and drugs to have a good time, but Benton explains that this is a misconception. She says, "Students are surprised to learn most of their classmates are not drinking to excess or using drugs. . . . About one out of five students does not drink at all. Excessive drinking is the exception, not the norm."[45] In addition, using these substances to help with psychological issues does not work and may lead to addiction.

Second, Benton reminds teens that physical and mental health are inextricably intertwined. She advises all teens to get good nutrition, exercise regularly, get enough sleep, and make time for friends and relaxation. Next, Benton emphasizes knowing when you need to ask for help. She says the first sign that stress, depression, or anxiety is becoming a problem is having trouble concentrating, especially on schoolwork, and that students need to be aware of this important sign and not ignore it. Finally, if efforts to improve mental health on your own are not effective, or if the problems continue for several months, Benton urges teens to seek professional help. She explains, "Most colleges and universities have a counseling service or offer a student assistance program that can help evaluate a student's situation and get them to the help most likely to be effective."[46]

Take Care of Yourself

As a college freshman, Meggan Montuori experienced firsthand the challenges of coping with mental health issues. She has an anxiety disorder, but she did complete her first year of college successfully. She approached the college's office of disability and asked for accommodations in her classes (such as taking exams in a separate room) to avoid situations that triggered anxiety. She also took advantage of the counseling services available at her

Alone in the Crowd

The American College Health Association conducted a survey of twenty-eight thousand students at fifty-one colleges around the country and found some surprising results. More than 60 percent of students had felt very lonely during the past year, and almost 30 percent had been that lonely in the two weeks prior to the survey. Many people do not realize how hard it can be for many young people to find comfortable social groups and make friends when they go to college. The trouble is that students do not know that others feel the same way. Students often don't admit their loneliness to each other. The feeling of being alone can be awful. Brett Epstein, for example, left his New York City high school friends to attend the College of Charleston in South Carolina. He recalls, "I spent my first night in the dorm and it hit me like a pile of bricks: It's just me here. I was completely freaked out." Sadness and loneliness are a normal part of adjusting to college that almost everyone just has to survive.

Quoted in Frank Bruni, "The Real Campus Scourge," *New York Times*, September 2, 2017. www.nytimes.com.

school. And she paid attention to her nutrition, exercise needs, and sleep scheduling. Her social anxiety was high, but Montuori pushed herself to make friends in her classes and in her dorm. She also kept in regular contact with her friends and family at home. And Montuori found some creative solutions for when her stress levels threatened to get out of control. She kept a journal to get the "million thoughts" out of her head and off her shoulders. She made a "comfort box" to soothe herself when things got rough. She explains, "A comfort box is so useful. . . . In my comfort box I kept adult coloring books, markers, colored pencils, my journal, favorite snacks, a stress ball, bubbles, a glitter jar, etc. You can really add whatever you want that may help you feel better."[47]

Montuori's ultimate advice is, "Take care of yourself and your mental health anyway you can."[48] It is good advice for everyone.

CHAPTER SIX

Risk Taking

One night in November 2018, Dallas teen Triston Bailey and a group of friends were driving home from a hockey game when they decided to pull over on the freeway bridge and take a dangerous selfie with the downtown skyline in the background. The eighteen-year-old explained later, "You see it all over social media. On Instagram and Facebook, people with really cool cameras. We wanted to have our own."[49] As he maneuvered and climbed around the concrete barriers on the edge of the bridge with his camera, looking for the perfect shot, Bailey slipped and fell 50 feet (15.2 m) to the ground below, landing so hard that he left the imprint of his body in the dirt.

Bailey does not remember the incident now at all, but his friends tell him he yelled and then slipped out of sight. He ended up in the hospital with serious injuries, and he was lucky, according to doctors, to be alive. He recalls, "I broke my pelvis, I had a rib fracture, a punctured lung, I broke my face a whole bunch and I had lacerated my spleen."[50] After four months of receiving medical treatment, being in a wheelchair and then on crutches, and undergoing physical therapy, Bailey is expected to make a full recovery, and he hopes his nearly fatal experience will serve as a warning to others that no photo is worth risking your life. According to one study, 259 people around the world died taking selfies from 2011 to 2017. Most of them have been young men.

Brains Craving Risks

Why are teens so often risk takers? Tim Elmore, a minister, author, and educator of young people in leadership skills, says that their brains program them to seek out risks. He explains:

> It's been a fact for years—during the period of adolescence, young people are prone to take more risks than at any other time of their life. The pre-frontal cortex is developing during this period. The portions of the brain attuned to reward for risks are very high and the portions of the brain that signal consequences for risk are very low. This can lead "smart kids to do some dumb things."[51]

Elmore does not mean than teens are unable to reason. As a matter of fact, a teen's ability to reason equals that of an adult. Rather, according to psychological research, the social-emotional part of the brain is just stronger during the teen years than the brain's cognitive control system. The cognitive control system is responsible for planning, weighing consequences, and self-regulating, and it continues to develop through early adulthood. So, teens are more likely to make impulsive, emotional decisions and to need to take risks for the stimulation they provide and the novel experiences that feel so rewarding as people are growing up.

The desire to test limits and stretch one's wings is an inherent part of the teenage years. Teens are searching for independence, the chance to gain experience in the world, the approval of their friendship groups, and ways to combat stress and to let off steam. They are determining the kind of person they want to be. Risk taking is not necessarily bad. Without the willingness to take risks, no one would try new things or make progress. Professor David

> "It's been a fact for years—during the period of adolescence, young people are prone to take more risks than at any other time of their life."[51]
>
> —Tim Elmore, minister and educator

Researchers say that because the portion of the brain that processes the consequences of actions is still developing in teens, they are more likely to engage in risky behavior.

Bainbridge of the University of Cambridge in the United Kingdom believes that risk taking is vital to the survival of the human race. As an example, he says, "If no one took any risks, you would never ask someone out and there would soon be no people left at all!"[52] The problem is not the propensity to take risks. The problem is ensuring that the risks taken are survivable. Teens need to use their reason to assess the dangers of risks and make wise choices about which risks are worth taking.

The CDC conducts a Youth Risk Behavior Survey every other year to assess the most dangerous risks that high schoolers commonly take. In 2017 it reported that 10 percent of students had four or more sexual partners (increasing the risk for unintended pregnancies and sexually transmitted diseases) and that only 54 percent of sexually active teens used condoms. (Overall, 40 percent of high schoolers were sexually active.) Fourteen percent of students reported using illegal drugs, such as heroin or hallucinogens, while one in seven abused opioids. In addition, 2.6 percent smoked cigarettes, 29.8 percent drank alcohol at least once in a thirty-day period, and 5.5 percent of students admitted to driving after drinking alcohol. Sixteen percent had ridden in a car with a driver who had been drinking, 5.9 percent rarely or never wore a seat belt when a passenger in a car, and 39.2 percent had texted or emailed while driving. Other dangerous risks included carrying some kind of weapon and getting into a physical fight. All these practices are considered by the CDC to be health-related and among the leading causes of death in young people.

Substance Misuse

Alcohol and drug use create a double risk. First, they are risky toxins in and of themselves that are best avoided because they interfere with normal brain development. Psychologist Laurence Steinberg of Temple University explains, "Adolescence is a time

Which Risks?

Although both male and female teenagers are drawn to taking risks, on average, they tend to exhibit different kinds of risky behaviors. Male teens, for example, may dare to draw graffiti in extreme places (such as in a railroad tunnel), drive their cars fast and recklessly, climb on top of a moving car or stand up through its sunroof, train surf (jump onto the outside of and ride a moving train), or get into a physical fight. One thrill-seeking Australian teen was killed when he risked being towed behind a carful of friends on his skateboard. Female teens, on the other hand, tend to risk activities like shoplifting, smoking, sneaking out of the house at night, joining friends to drink in the park, or accepting spontaneous dares from friends. For both genders, the likelihood of engaging in dangerous risk taking doubles when they are in a group of peers.

when the parts of the brain that are particularly sensitive to recreational drugs are still developing." The brain's reward system is especially affected, and teens who use drugs and alcohol before age fifteen are ten times more likely to develop a substance abuse problem or addiction than those who wait to experiment until they are twenty-one. Scientists are unsure of the exact age that trying drugs is less dangerous. Steinberg says, "Delaying it to 18 or later is going to be very important. Whether it makes a difference to delay it after 18 is something we don't yet know."[53] The longer you delay trying these drugs, however, the healthier your brain will be long term.

> "Adolescence is a time when the parts of the brain that are particularly sensitive to recreational drugs are still developing."[53]
>
> —Laurence Steinberg, psychologist

The other problem with drugs and alcohol is that they increase the likelihood that you will engage in other risky activities, such as smoking or driving while under the influence. Alcohol and drugs simply impair judgment, no matter what your age. While under their influence people do all sorts of things that they normally would not do. Alcohol and drugs can also worsen mental health issues, such as depression, and perhaps increase the possibility of self-harm or suicidal thoughts.

Behind the Wheel

Vehicle accidents are the leading cause of death in teens, sometimes because of drinking or drug use, but often just because of distraction or risk taking. California mom Bonnye Spray lost her teenage daughter Amanda Clark to a distracted driving accident in 2007. Since that time, Spray has dedicated her life to telling teens her story and urging them to put their phones away when they are driving. The accident that took Clark's life was her second. In 2006 she was talking on her phone, ran a stop sign, and was struck by another car. Her vehicle rolled three times, but Clark survived the accident with just bruises and scrapes. Afterward,

A Tragedy for So Many

Michael Anderson is still haunted by the day his train hit and killed three girls taking selfies on the tracks. The train engineer begs other teens not to take such risks. He says, "I'd tell them to stay away from such a dangerous area. Think about the pain it would inflict on their families if things went wrong. It also hurts the train crew, the first responders and the many people who love you."

On one awful day in October 2011 in Spanish Fork Canyon, Utah, fifteen-year-old Essa Ricker, fifteen-year-old Kelsea Webster, and Kelsea's thirteen-year-old sister, Savannah, stood between two railroad tracks as a westbound train rushed past. Facing the direction from which the train came, they snapped a happy, excited selfie and posted on Facebook, "Standing right by a train ahaha this is awesome!!!!" Grinning and windblown, they were completely oblivious to what was behind them. An eastbound train's headlights appear over their shoulders in the photo. The girls never heard Anderson's oncoming train because of the noise from the first. The terrified engineer blasted the horn and slammed on the emergency brakes, uselessly screaming for the girls to move. Anderson could not prevent the catastrophe that took those three lives.

Quoted in Inside Track, "Selfie Tragedy Forever Impacts Those Left Behind," December 8, 2016. www.up.com.

Clark vowed to put her phone away while driving. She wrote in a school essay, "I believe everything happens for a reason and the reason for my car accident is to let me know that I need to slow down and pay more attention. I know that I need to change the way I have been living my life. My phone and talking to my friends put me in danger. I realize how easy it is for my life to be over because I wasn't paying attention."[54] That wisdom did not last.

A year later, Clark was killed when she lost control of her car. At the time of the crash, she was texting with her roommate. Her mother says now that "it was for a short time she wouldn't talk on the phone, she was more cautious. But she got more confident in her driving and a sense of 'Hey, I survived one, I'm invincible, nothing is going to happen to me now.'"[55] Spray pleads with other teens not to make the same mistake.

Dumb, Useless Dares

A willingness to take negligent risks, like texting while driving, is one way teens can put themselves in danger, but many times, teens also indulge in extreme risks on purpose—to test their limits, for excitement and brain stimulation, and sometimes to impress other teens. These risks often take the form of Internet or social media challenges or dares from friendship groups. Community college student Caitlyn Conville ponders some of these most extreme challenges, those that carry high risk of death or injury, and simply concludes, "Don't be an idiot."[56] One such challenge involves jumping out of a moving car. An eighteen-year-old who tried this—Anna Worden—fell, hit her head, and fractured her skull. She lived but has to relearn to walk because of brain injuries. Other teens have accepted the challenge to set themselves on fire (a stunt first uploaded on the Internet in 2012), cut off their oxygen in the "choking game" in an attempt to get high, and swallowing a spoonful of cinnamon (which can lead to permanent respiratory issues and lung problems).

The issue of extreme pranks and dares causing harm to people has become so pervasive that YouTube banned such challenges and dares from its platform in 2019 if they are judged to encourage dangerous activities. Whether you are dared to eat Tide Pods or put salt and ice on your skin or any other stupid antic, stop and think first. Ignore these kinds of challenges and tricks. You cannot live a healthy lifestyle if you are not alive or are spending months recovering from an injury.

Positive Risk Taking

Teens seeking new experiences and wanting to take risks can find positive ways to meet those needs. According to science writer Kayt Sukel, brain development and the desire for risk taking

Experts say that teens can indulge their natural desire for taking risks by participating in activities that are challenging and exciting but not dangerous.

"allow for unprecedented learning and skill-building. Taking those risks is critical to helping teens gain the experience they need to grow up and make their way in the world."[57] Sukel just advises that the risks be relatively safe.

Healthy risk taking, for example, might include performing on-stage in front of an audience, playing new sports, or traveling to new places. It could also involve volunteering for a social or political cause, riding the scariest roller coaster, or participating in outdoor adventures such as wilderness camps or Outward Bound (an outdoor learning and skill-building program offering challenging wilderness expeditions). Taking risks that help you develop competency and independence can be a strong component of a healthy lifestyle.

SOURCE NOTES

Introduction: What Is a Healthy Lifestyle?

1. World Health Organization, "Constitution," *Basic Documents*, 45th ed., Supplement, October 2006. www.who.int.
2. Chris Hudson, "It's Official: Ravenous Teenage Boys are 'Normal,'" Understanding Boys, May 30, 2016. www.understandingboys.com.au.
3. Quoted in Michael O. Schroeder, "Why Teens Should Be Heart Healthy, Too," *U.S. News & World Report*, August 28, 2018. https://health.usnews.com.
4. NIH Osteoporosis and Related Bone Diseases National Resource Center, "Kids and Their Bones: A Guide for Parents," March 2015. www.bones.nih.gov.
5. Thomas G. Plante, "Health Habits Develop Early and Are Hard to Change," *Psychology Today*, May 29, 2012. www.psychologytoday.com.

Chapter One: Nutrition and a Healthy Diet

6. American Academy of Child & Adolescent Psychiatry, "Teen Brain: Behavior, Problem Solving, and Decision Making," 2016. www.aacap.org.
7. Quoted in Samantha Costa, "Teens, Your Brain Needs Real Food," *U.S. News & World Report*, January 5, 2016. https://health.usnews.com.
8. Quoted in Costa, "Teens, Your Brain Needs Real Food."
9. Quoted in Costa, "Teens, Your Brain Needs Real Food."
10. Alissa Rumsey, "Why Is There So Much Confusion over Nutrition?," *Alissa Rumsey Nutrition and Wellness* (blog), July 18, 2017. https://alissarumsey.com.
11. Amy Reichelt, "Teens: Your Brain on Junk Food," *Food for Thought* (blog), NeuroTrition. https://neurotrition.ca.
12. Reichelt, "Teens."
13. SafeTeens.org, "Dieting the Healthy Way," 2019. https://safeteens.org.

Chapter Two: Grocery Shopping and Cooking

14. Faith Branch, "What I Wish I'd Known About Grocery Shopping Before I Went to College," Spoon University, 2018. https://spoonuniversity.com.
15. Sara Ipatenco, "How to Avoid Bad Foods When Grocery Shopping," SFGate, 2018. https://healthyeating.sfgate.com.
16. Quoted in Heidi Stevens, "Grocery Aisles Full of Lessons for Teens," *Chicago Tribune*, February 27, 2013. www.chicagotribune.com.
17. Branch, "What I Wish I'd Known About Grocery Shopping Before I Went to College."
18. Casey Clark, "I Tried Cooking for the First Time and This Is What Happened," Spoon University, 2018. https://spoonuniversity.com.

19. Clark, "I Tried Cooking for the First Time and This Is What Happened."
20. Michael C. '16, "The Starving Student's Guide to Cooking for Yourself," *MIT Admissions* (blog), January 28, 2013. https://mitadmissions.org.
21. Michael C. '16, "The Starving Student's Guide to Cooking for Yourself."

Chapter Three: Physical Activity
22. Centers for Disease Control and Prevention, "Physical Activity Facts," April 9, 2018. www.cdc.gov.
23. Centers for Disease Control and Prevention, "Physical Activity Facts."
24. Jesse Calestine et al., "College Student Work Habits Are Related to Physical Activity and Fitness," *International Journal of Exercise Science*, November 1, 2017, p. 1014. www.ncbi.nlm.nih.gov.
25. Elizabeth Oliver, "Strategies to Incorporate Physical Activity as a College Student." UCDavis Student Health and Counseling Services, May 14, 2016. https://shcs.ucdavis.edu.
26. Quoted in Oliver, "Strategies to Incorporate Physical Activity as a College Student."
27. Tina Ma, "A Story of Sports," Sutter Health, Palo Alto Medical Foundation, 2013. www.pamf.org.
28. Ma, "A Story of Sports."
29. Canadian Society for Exercise Physiology, "Physical Activity Tips for Youth (12–17 years)," Government of Canada, October 1, 2018. www.canada.ca.
30. National Institute of Diabetes and Digestive and Kidney Diseases, "Take Charge of Your Health: A Guide for Teenagers," 2016. www.niddk.nih.gov.
31. Quoted in Vanessa Brown, "16-Year-Old Sydney Student Reveals Stunning Transformation After Shedding 65kg," News.com.au, June 13, 2017. www.news.com.au.

Chapter Four: Sleep
32. National Sleep Foundation, "Teens and Sleep," 2019. www.sleepfoundation.org.
33. Quoted in Rick Nauert, "Teens' Sleep Deprivation Tied to Poor Diet, Obesity," Psych Central, August 8, 2018. https://psychcentral.com.
34. Mary A. Carskadon, "Sleep and Teens—Biology and Behavior," National Sleep Foundation, 2006. www.sleepfoundation.org.
35. Carskadon, "Sleep and Teens—Biology and Behavior."
36. National Sleep Foundation, "How Blue Light Affects Kids & Sleep," 2019. www.sleepfoundation.org.
37. Shawn A. Clark, "Blue Light Blocking Glasses for College Students," CollegeWisdom, 2019. https://thecollegewisdom.com.
38. Jennie Miremadi, "How to Manage Stress," *Chalkboard*, September 11, 2017. https://thechalkboardmag.com.
39. Maryellen Fitzgerald-Bord, "How to Survive with No Sleep," *Student Voices* (blog), Utica College, March 29, 2014. www.utica.edu.

Chapter Five: Social and Psychological Health

40. Quoted in Megan Scudellari, "Study Says That a Social Life Is a Healthy Life," *Boston Globe*, January 26, 2016. www.bostonglobe.com.
41. Golden Goose Award, "2016: A Tale of Two Studies: The Adolescent Health Story." www.goldengooseaward.org.
42. Quoted in Joanne Van Zuidam, "7 Things No One Tells You About Making Friends in College," Course Hero, September 20, 2018. www.coursehero.com.
43. Ransom Patterson, "How to Make Friends in College: A Comprehensive Guide," College Info Geek, August 17, 2017. https://collegeinfogeek.com.
44. Teen Talk, "Mental Health." http://teentalk.ca.
45. Quoted in Abigail Hess, "Massive Survey Finds 1 in 3 College Freshmen Struggle with Mental Health—Here Are 4 Things You Can Do," CNBC Make It, October 4, 2018. www.cnbc.com.
46. Quoted in Hess, "Massive Survey Finds 1 in 3 College Freshmen Struggle with Mental Health—Here Are 4 Things You Can Do."
47. Meggan Montuori, "14 Tips on Surviving College with Anxiety," *Mighty* (blog), September 3, 2017. https://themighty.com.
48. Montuori, "14 Tips on Surviving College with Anxiety."

Chapter Six: Risk Taking

49. Quoted in Callum Paton, "Texas Teen Nearly Dies After Selfie Gone Wrong, Plummets 50 Feet off Bridge: 'I Broke My Face a Whole Bunch,'" *Newsweek*, February 21, 2019. www.newsweek.com.
50. Quoted in Paton, "Texas Teen Nearly Dies After Selfie Gone Wrong, Plummets 50 Feet Off Bridge."
51. Tim Elmore, "The Role of Risk in a Teen's Life," *Artificial Maturity* (blog), *Psychology Today*, January 2, 2014. www.psychologytoday.com.
52. Quoted in Ann Robinson, "Is Teenage Risk-Taking Vital for Our Species?," *Guardian* (Manchester), October 19, 2015. www.theguardian.com.
53. Quoted in Diana Simeon, "Alcohol, Drugs, and the Teenage Brain (and What You Can Do)," *Your Teen*, 2019. https://yourteenmag.com.
54. Quoted in Erin Tracy, "She Survived Her First Distracted Driving Accident—but Not Her Second," *Charlotte (NC) Observer*, December 21, 2016. www.charlotteobserver.com.
55. Quoted in Tracy, "She Survived Her First Distracted Driving Accident—but Not Her Second."
56. Caitlyn Conville, "The 5 Most Dangerous Internet Challenges: And a Million Reasons Never to Try Them," *Study Breaks*, September 9, 2018. https://studybreaks.com.
57. Quoted in Stacy Lu, "Why Teens Need to Take Risks—and How to Help Them Be Smart About It," *Life* (blog), HuffPost, July 20, 2016. www.huffpost.com.

FOR MORE INFORMATION

Books

Eliana de Las Casas, *Teen Chef Cooks: 80 Scrumptious Family-Friendly Recipes*. Emmaus, PA: Rodale, 2019.

Christie Garton, *U Chic: The College Girl's Guide to Everything*. Naperville, IL: Sourcebooks, 2017.

Allison Krumsiek, *Teens and Alcohol: A Dangerous Combination*. New York: Lucent, 2019.

Nicola Morgan, *Positively Teen: A Practical Guide to a More Positive, More Confident You*. New York: Poppy, Hachette, 2019.

Paula Nagel, *The Mental Health and Wellbeing Workout for Teens: Skills and Exercises from ACT and CBT for Healthy Thinking*. Philadelphia: Kingsley, 2019.

Amy Newmark, *Chicken Soup for the Soul: Think Positive for Teens*. Cos Cob, CT: Chicken Soup for the Soul, 2019.

Danielle Sherman-Lazar, *Living FULL: Winning My Battle with Eating Disorders*. Coral Gables, FL: Mango, 2018.

Internet Sources

William Butler, "43 Cool Recipes for Teens to Make at Home," DIY Projects for Teens, November 19, 2016. https://diyprojectsforteens.com.

FamilyDoctor.org Editorial Staff, "Teenagers: How to Stay Healthy," American Academy of Family Physicians, July 6, 2017. https://familydoctor.org.

Angela Oswalt, "Healthy Teens: Exercise and Sports," Mental Help.net. www.mentalhelp.net.

Websites

ChooseMyPlate.gov (www.choosemyplate.gov/MyPlatePlan). The USDA's MyPlate Plan provides personalized recommendation for an individual's dietary needs. Find out what and how much teens need of different foods to live a healthy nutritional lifestyle.

SafeTeens.org (https://safeteens.org). This comprehensive website offers tips and advice on all aspects of living a safe and healthy lifestyle. Explore topics such as health and wellness, physical fitness, dating and relationships, bullying, and substance abuse.

Spoon University (https://spoonuniversity.com). At this very large website, by and for college students, visitors and members can explore food advice, cookbooks, lifestyle advice from other students, and much more.

Study Breaks (https://studybreaks.com). *Study Breaks* is magazine and a website designed and written by college students nationwide. It is devoted to the thoughts and stories of interest to college people, whether creative, advice oriented, or about pop culture. The site offers many lifestyle articles, from mental health tips to cooking to relationship advice.

Teen Talk (http://teentalk.ca). This Canadian Youth Health Education Program explains that it offers facts and information to help teens make their own health decisions about their bodies. It covers topics as varied as sexuality, substance abuse, diversity and discrimination, mental health, and eating disorders.

INDEX

PICTURE CREDITS

ABOUT THE AUTHOR

Toney Allman holds a BS in psychology from Ohio State University and an MA in clinical psychology from the University of Hawaii. She currently lives in Virginia, where she enjoys a rural lifestyle and researching and writing about a variety of topics for students.